Diet and the cancer patient

This booklet may be helpful for you, if you have or someone close to you has cancer. Cancer, and the treatments for it, may make eating difficult or may mean you have to think more carefully about your diet. If you are a patient, your doctor or nurse may wish to go through the booklet with you and mark sections that are particularly important for you. You can make a note below of the main contacts and information that you may need quickly.

Specialist nurse/dietitian names

....

....

Hospital

....

....

....

Phone ....

Treatments ....

....

....

Family doctor

....

....

Surgery address

....

....

....

Phone ....

Review dates..................

....

....

If you like, you can also add:

Your name ....

Address ....

D1342385

cancerBACUP

Helping people live with cancer

3 Bath Place, Rivington Street, London EC2A 3DR

CancerBACUP was founded by Dr Vicky Clement-Jones, following her own experiences with ovarian cancer, and offers information, counselling and support to people with cancer, their families and friends.

We produce publications on the main types of cancer, treatments, and ways of living with cancer. We also produce a magazine, *CancerBACUP News*, three times a year.

Our success depends on feedback from users of the service. We thank everyone, particularly patients and their families, whose advice has made this booklet possible.

Administration 0171 696 9003
Cancer Support Service:
Information 0171 613 2121 (8 lines) or Freeline 0800 18 11 99
Counselling 0171 696 9000 (London)
CancerBACUP Scotland Cancer Counselling Service
0141 553 1553 (Glasgow)

British Association of Cancer United Patients and their families and friends. A company limited by guarantee. Registered in England and Wales company number 2803321. Charity registration number 1019719. Registered office 3 Bath Place, Rivington Street, London, EC2A 3DR

Medical consultant: Dr Maurice Slevin, MD, FRCP

Editor: Stella Wood

Cover design: Rob Martin Associates

Cover photo: The Image Bank

Illustrations: Belinda Blake

CancerBACUP thanks Anne Allbright RN, Susan Parkinson NSc and Mary Venn RN for their help writing the original text of this booklet

©CancerBACUP 1987, 1989, 1992, 1994, 1995, 1996, 1997, 1998
First published 1987, 3rd revised edition published 1992, reprinted 1994, 1995 (twice), revised 1996, 1997, reprinted 1998

All rights reserved. No part of this publication may be reproduced or transmitted, in any form or by any means, electronic or mechanical, including photocopying, recording or any information storage and retrieval system, without permission in writing from CancerBACUP.

Typeset and printed in Great Britain by Lithoflow Ltd., London

ISBN 1-870403-97-5

Contents

Introduction   4

PART ONE: *The building-up diet*   6

How to boost your energy and protein   10
How to add extra energy and protein to everyday foods   12
Table of commercial supplements available   14
Nourishing drinks   18
Sample menus   21
Your feelings about weight loss   24

PART TWO: *Eating problems*   27

Sore mouth   27
Dry mouth   29
Has your taste changed?   30
Too tired to cook or eat   31
Constipation   32
Diarrhoea   33
Wind   34
Feeling sick   35
Difficulty in chewing or swallowing   36
Poor appetite   37
Special eating problems   38

PART THREE: *A healthy eating guide*   39

Watch your weight   40
Eat less fat   40
Eat more vegetables, fruit and cereals   41
Cut down on sugar   42
Cut down on salt   42
What about alternative diets for treating cancer?   43
Recommended cookery books   44
Manufacturers of nutritional products   45
CancerBACUP's services   46
CancerBACUP booklets   47

Introduction

Food contributes much to the quality of our lives and is more than just a physical need. Mealtimes are an important and enjoyable part of family and social life.

Many people with cancer experience eating problems. This booklet is divided into three parts and is intended to help you overcome these difficulties. If you find it hard to discuss your eating problems with your family or friends, you may like to give them this booklet to read so they can help you with your diet.

Part One, **The building-up diet,** is a diet high in energy and protein and has been designed specifically for people with cancer who have lost or are losing weight or can only manage to eat a little. We do not recommend this diet for people with cancer who are eating well and have not lost weight.

Part Two, **Eating problems,** has helpful hints for people with cancer who have temporary eating problems caused by their disease or treatment. For example, you may be feeling sick, have mouth ulcers or be too tired to cook a normal meal.

Part Three, **A healthy eating guide,** is for people with cancer who do not have eating or weight loss problems, but would like to follow a healthy diet.

Information on diet as part of complementary therapy is included in CancerBACUP's booklet *Cancer and complementary therapies.*

If you have any problems that are not covered by this booklet, please do not hesitate to discuss them with your doctor, nurse, dietitian or CancerBACUP's cancer information service.

PART ONE
The building-up diet

Many people with cancer find there are times when they cannot eat as much as usual and sometimes they lose weight. There are lots of reasons why this happens.

Cancer itself or its treatment may cause you to lose your appetite. Some people do not feel hungry or feel full soon after starting a meal. Others find that food makes them feel sick or they notice a change in the taste of some foods.

People who are not eating enough, especially those who are losing weight, need more energy and protein in their diet. This section of the booklet will show you how to get more energy and protein without necessarily having to eat more food. Not everyone will be able to put on weight with this building-up diet, but the suggestions should help to slow down or stop weight loss.

A good diet is one that provides you with everything you need to keep your body working well. The key to a good diet is variety and balance. You should try to include everyday foods from each of the groups described on the next page.

'Many people with cancer find there are times when they cannot eat as much as usual'

s, rice, pasta, breakfast cereals,
, biscuits and sweets are carbohydrate
es which provide energy, fibre,
ns and minerals. Wholemeal and whole
varieties are especially high in fibre.

fruit and fresh
ables are good sources
amins, minerals and
Eaten raw or lightly
ed, with skins on when
cal, they retain more
ins.

poultry, fish, beans,
, nuts, eggs, milk and
e are protein sources
provide vitamins,
als and energy as well.

utter, margarine, fatty meats, oily fish,
cheese, cream, nuts, salad dressing and
nnaise, full-fat milk, yogurts and
ge frais are fat sources which also
e protein, vitamins and energy.

ake sure that eggs are well cooked; use commercial, not home-made
nnaise. Avoid soft cheese like Brie, and cheeses made from unpasteurised milk. This is
se these foods carry a risk of infection.

Energy

Energy is measured in *calories,* so a calorie is simply a unit of energy. We all need a certain number of calories each day to provide the energy to live. We need energy even if we are not very active; just sitting in a chair we need energy to breathe. On the whole, if there are too many calories in our diet we gain weight and if there are too few, we start to use up our body's stores of energy and lose weight.

Proteins

Proteins make up the basic building blocks of the body. Every part of the body is made up of protein and we need to eat protein every day to maintain and repair our body tissues. The body must have extra protein, as well as extra energy, when we are ill, injured or under stress in order to repair any damage.

Vitamins

Vitamins are essential substances which help our bodies to work normally, but we only need tiny amounts of them. If you are eating even a little of the main foods that contain vitamins, you are probably getting a good enough supply. However, if you are not eating well over a long period of time, you may need a multivitamin tablet to top up your body's stores. Your doctor, dietitian or pharmacist at your local chemist can advise you about these.

There is no scientific evidence to prove that taking large amounts of vitamins is helpful. In fact it can be harmful to take excessive amounts of certain vitamins, especially Vitamins A and D.

'We need energy
even if we are
not very active'

How to boost your energy and protein

If you have a good appetite, you should have no trouble eating extra energy and protein foods to fortify your diet. But if you have a poor appetite, there are two ways to add extra energy and protein to your diet, without actually having to eat more food.

The first is to use everyday foods high in energy and protein, and the second is to use manufactured food supplements. These can be taken as nourishing drinks and/or added to your normal food.

Using everyday foods high in energy and protein

Pages 12 & 13 give you some simple ideas on how to do this.

Manufactured food supplements

Important note:

High protein supplements should only be used with advice from your doctor or dietitian. Most people will need extra energy with a balance of protein.

Many of these products can be used by diabetics. Complete milk-tasting drinks and powders should be drunk slowly over a period of 20 minutes.

BANANA
MILKSHAKE

HOCOLATE
LKSHAKE

STRAWBERRY

High-energy and juice-tasting supplements have a high carbohydrate (sugar) content and are therefore not usually suitable for diabetics.

If you are a diabetic you should always seek advice from your doctor or dietitian before using food supplements.

There are many commercially available supplements which can add extra energy and/or protein to your diet. They are usually available from your chemist. Some are available on prescription from your doctor. Some supplements are available ready to drink or use and others need mixing. Some can be added to food. A list of these products can be found on pages 14-16.

Fortified milk

Add 2 tablespoonfuls of dried milk powder to a pint (60cl) of full-cream milk. Keep in the fridge and use in drinks and cooking. Use fortified milk, Fortisip Neutral or Entera Neutral instead of water to make up soups, jellies, custard and puddings.

Breakfast cereals

Use fortified milk. Add syrup or honey to porridge or use 2-3 teaspoons of a high-energy supplement e.g. Polycal Powder, Maxijul or Polycose instead of sugar or salt. Make porridge with all milk or cream.

Casseroles and soups

Add lentils, beans and noodles. Stir a tablespoon of cream into canned soups or add energy and protein supplements. Make up packet soups with fortified milk or a milk-tasting supplement e.g. Fortisip Neutral or Entera Neutral.

Nibbles

Keep snacks like nuts, crisps, fresh and dried fruit, biscuits, crackers, yogurts or fromage frais handy to nibble if you feel hungry between meals.

Puddings

Add ice cream, cream or evaporated milk to cold puddings, and custard made with fortified milk to hot puddings. Make up instant desserts with fortified milk. Try adding sugar or syrup to puddings. Alternatively try some pudding recipes for use with Fortisip, Ensure Plus or Entera.

shed potato

ed potato can be enriched by adding a
rtspoon of butter or cream, or a supplement
as Polycal Powder, Vitajoule or Caloreen,
y sprinkling grated cheese on top. High-
y and protein supplements can be
i.

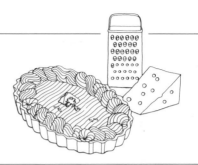

etables

utter on top of hot vegetables or
sh with grated cheese or chopped
oiled egg. Alternatively, serve with a
made with fortified milk.

dwiches

d fillings thickly. Add a dessertspoon
yonnaise to sandwich fillings like
oiled egg, or tuna fish.

nks

ortified milk, or half milk instead of
when making coffee and bedtime
s. Add three teaspoonfuls of a high-
y supplement to hot or cold drinks. Commercial
s can be drunk straight from the pack, gently
d or incorporated into recipes.

Table of commercial supplements available

PRODUCT	PRESENTATION	MANUFACTURER
READY TO DRINK:		
COMPLETE HIGH-ENERGY, MILK-TASTING: (i)		
Fortisip	200ml carton (fruit, savoury, neutral and dessert)	Nutricia Clinical Care
Ensure Plus	200ml carton (sweet)	Ross Products Division
Entera	200ml carton (sweet, savoury and neutral)	Fresenius Ltd
YOGURT-TASTING: (i)		
Fortifresh	200ml carton (sweet)	Nutricia Clinical Care
BALANCED, JUICE-TASTING: (i)		
Fortijuce	200ml carton	Nutricia Clinical Care
Enlive	240ml carton	Ross Products Division
Provide Xtra	250ml carton	Fresenius Ltd
OTHERS – MILK-TASTING: (i)		
Fortimel (high protein)	200ml carton	Nutricia Clinical Care
Ensure	250ml can	Ross Products Division
Protein Forte (high protein)	200ml carton	Fresenius Ltd
Fresubin	200ml carton	Fresenius Ltd

PRODUCT	PRESENTATION	MANUFACTURER
POWDERS:		
ENERGY-ONLY POWDERS: **(ii)**		
Polycal Powder	400g tin	Nutricia Clinical Care
Maxijul	Box 4 x 140g sachet	SHS International Ltd
Polycose	350g tin	Ross Products Division
Vitajoule	125g tub	Vitaflo Ltd
Caloreen	250g bottle	Nestlé Clinical Nutrition
PROTEIN-ONLY POWDERS: **(iii)**		
Protifar	225g tub	Nutricia Clinical Care
Maxipro	200g tub	SHS International Ltd
Vitapro	250g tub	Vitaflo Ltd
COMPLETE, MILK-TASTING: **(iv)**		
Complan	Box 6 x 58g sachet (sweet and savoury)	H J Heinz & Co Ltd
Build-Up	38g sachet (sweet and savoury)	Nestlé Clinical Nutrition
ENERGY-ONLY LIQUID: **(iv)**		
Polycal Liquid	200ml bottle	Nutricia Clinical Care
Calsip	200ml carton	Fresenius Ltd
Maxijul Liquid	200ml carton	SHS International Ltd

Table of semi-solid supplements available

PRODUCT	PRESENTATION	MANUFACTURER
FORTIFIED PUDDINGS: (v)		
Fortipudding	150g tub	Nutricia Clinical Care
Formance	142g tin	Ross Products Division
Maxisorb	30g sachet (to make up)	SHS International Ltd
Emelis	125g tub	Nestlé Clinical Nutrition
POWDERS TO THICKEN FOOD: (vi)		
Nutilis	225g tin	Nutricia Clinical Care
Instant Carobel	45g packet	Cow & Gate
Thick and Easy	225g tin	Fresenius Ltd
Thixo-D	375g tin	Sutherland Health Ltd
Vitaquick	250g tub	Vitaflo Ltd
Nestargel	125g packet	Nestlé Clinical Nutrition

Key for table, pages 14-16

(i) These contain energy, protein and vitamins and minerals in various amounts. Available in a variety of flavours to suit individual tastes they can be used as additional nutrition or added to recipes – see sample menus for ideas.

(ii) These contain energy only and have no taste. These can be added to normal foods – see suggestions on pages 12 and 19.

(iii) These contain protein only and have no taste. These can be added to normal foods – see suggestions on page 19.

(iv) These contain energy only and are available in a variety of flavours to suit individual tastes. Can be used as additional nutrition or added to recipes etc.

(v) These can be used to provide extra energy and protein instead of ordinary puddings.

(vi) These can be used to thicken drinks and foods for people who have difficulty in swallowing fluids. Follow the instructions carefully or products can become lumpy.

Recipe ideas, leaflets and booklets are available for many of these products from the manufacturers.

For a list of manufacturers and addresses see page 45.

Nourishing drinks

If you sometimes cannot face a meal, have a nourishing drink instead. You can also drink these between meals to help put on some weight. Some people like an occasional glass of Guinness or stout to help their appetite, or you might like to make your own drinks such as fruit milkshakes.

To make a nutritious milkshake, mix fortified milk with either puréed fruit or a fruit yogurt and add 2-3 teaspoonfuls of a high-energy powder supplement. A scoop of ice cream will top it off tastily, and add extra energy.

Ready to drink/use supplements

You may find it easier to buy a ready to drink, flavoured supplement from your chemist. Your doctor can also offer you a prescription for them. Supplements such as Fortisip, Fortifresh, Ensure Plus and Entera, or Fortijuce, Enlive and Provide Xtra are nutritionally balanced, so occasionally you can have one of them instead of a meal if you do not feel like eating. Supplements such as Polycal Liquid, Calsip or Maxijul Liquid are energy-only drinks. You will find the full list in the table on pages 14-16.

Powdered drinks

Other balanced and flavoured meal drinks are available as powders which can be mixed with milk or water (e.g. Build-Up or Complan). These can be bought from your chemist and from some supermarkets.

Powders which can be added to food

There are also unflavoured powders available to buy or on prescription. Energy-only powders include Polycal Powder, Maxijul or Polycose. Protein-only powders include Protifar, Maxipro or Vitapro. You will find the full list in the table on pages 14-16.

Since these powders are virtually tasteless you can add them to drinks, soups, sauces, gravies, casseroles, flan fillings, milk puddings and instant desserts made with liquids.

You will probably need to experiment a little to find out how much you can add to each particular dish without changing the flavour or texture of your food. A good way to start is to add 2-3 tablespoons of a powdered protein supplement such as Protifar, Maxipro or

Vitapro to a pint (60cl) of full-cream milk. Alternatively 2-3 teaspoons of an energy supplement such as Polycal Powder, Vitajoule or Caloreen can be added to a cup of tea or coffee. Energy supplements are almost flavourless and are not as sweet as sugar.

In the following pages we have taken some everyday foods and put them into sample menus to show how you can increase your protein and energy intake without having to eat more food.

Obviously these are only suggestions but we hope they will give you some ideas for ways you can adapt the meals you usually eat.

Between meals you can keep up your energy intake with snacks and drinks (see pages 12 and 18). Don't forget to add fortified milk or supplements such as Fortisip Neutral or Entera Neutral to tea and coffee. Use them to make bedtime drinks such as Horlicks, Ovaltine or drinking chocolate. Add energy supplements to hot drinks too.

Menu 1

make with fortified milk; add sugar or honey

spread thickly

Breakfast

fruit or fruit juice
porridge
toast with butter and jam or h[...]

add mayonnaise, generous filling

use full-fat variety; add energy supplement

Midday meal

cheese and salad sandwich wit[...]
wholemeal bread
fruit yogurt or fromage frais

add butter to vegetables

with syrup and ice cream, cream or custard made with fortified milk

Evening meal

roast chicken with fresh vegetables
fruit salad

Menu 2

Breakfast

fruit juice
puri (small chapati fried in oil) with potato bhaji

add energy and protein supplement

add butter

use butter for cooking

make with fortified milk and energy supplement

Midday meal

rice or chapati, vegetable curry, hard-boiled egg and potato curry, lentil soup
fruit or rice pudding

Evening meal

stuffed paratha or chapati with vegetables
lamb curry with pulses and salad
fruit custard with fresh cream

fry in oil or butter

Breakfast

add energy and protein supplements

fresh fruit juice or piece of fruit

spread thickly

wholemeal bread with butter and honey or jam

Midday meal

sprinkle cheese on soup

vegetable soup with wholemeal bread

add dressing, mayonnaise or salad cream

salad

made with fortified milk and energy supplement

egg custard

Evening meal

use fortified milk for sauce

grilled fish, potatoes, broccoli in cheese sauce

ice cream and fresh fruit

Breakfast

Weetabix

use fortified milk and sprinkle with sugar

toast with butter and jam

spread butter while still warm

Midday meal

add cream or energy and protein supplement

chicken soup

be generous with the filling add mayonnaise

hard-boiled egg sandwich

fruit or full-fat yogurt

serve with butter

use fortified mashed potato or grate cheese on top

Evening meal

shepherd's pie with carrots and peas

stewed fruit

serve with cream or custard made with fortified milk

Your feelings about weight loss

Weight loss is something that often happens to people who have cancer and many find it upsetting because it reminds them they are ill. This is a normal reaction, as over the years we all develop an image in our minds about what our bodies look like. Although we may not be completely satisfied with this image, most people do come to terms with the way they see themselves.

When you lose weight, perhaps as a result of the cancer itself or maybe the treatment you are receiving, you will see a different image of yourself when you look in the mirror from the one you have developed in your mind. It can be hard for someone who has seen themselves as well-built and robust, to accept that they now look different because they have lost weight.

You may also worry that the change in your looks will affect what your partner, family and friends think of you. But although you see yourself differently, and perhaps may think you are less attractive, it does not mean that others think the same. Despite your loss of weight, you are still the same person with the characteristics for which your family and friends value you.

Some people fear the change in their looks will affect their personal relationships. You may be worried about rejection or carrying on a sexual relationship. Many find, once they have summoned up the courage to talk openly to their partner, their fears of rejection are unfounded. Intimate relationships are built on a number of things – love, trust, common experiences and so many other feelings. You may even find a new closeness after working through the problem together.

People who have lost their appetites may feel self-conscious about eating at home with the family or eating out with friends. Eating is usually a social event, so even if you feel you cannot manage a full meal, there is no reason for you to feel excluded. Your friends and family will understand and will enjoy being with you, even if you can't eat as much as usual.

Sometimes, perhaps when you are feeling tired or sick, you may not be able to prepare food. If you are the person in your family who usually makes the meals, it can feel strange to stand back and let someone else take charge. It is important not to feel guilty about letting someone else do your tasks when you are unwell. After all, when you feel better again you can always take up your responsibility for cooking once more.

If you live alone and need help with cooking, or around the house generally, contact your GP, district nurse or social worker, so that they can arrange for a home help, meals-on-wheels or a local organisation to help with the cooking or shopping. You can always contact CancerBACUP for details of organisations that offer help in your area.

Don't hesitate to seek professional help if you are finding it difficult to cope with your illness and your emotions. Talking about your feelings can often help to clarify your own thoughts and give others the opportunity to understand how you are feeling. You may find it helpful to talk to a professional counsellor who lives near you or a local support group.

Don't see it as a sign of failure that you have not been able to cope on your own. Once people understand how you are feeling they can be more supportive.

PART TWO
Eating problems

Apart from a poor appetite and loss of weight, some people with cancer experience other difficulties with eating. Some of these problems may be related to the disease itself, while others may be temporary side effects of treatment.

In this section some of the possible difficulties are discussed and some suggestions are given to help you overcome them.

Sore mouth

● Drink plenty of nourishing fluids (see page 18). If you find fresh fruit juices sting your mouth, try drinking blackcurrant or rose hip syrup, apple juice or peach or pear nectar instead as these are less acidic. Some pre-prepared, juice-tasting drinks (see page 14) may also be helpful.

● Cold foods and drinks can be soothing to a sore mouth. Try adding crushed ice to drinks and eating ice cream or soft milk jellies.

● Avoid salty or spicy food which may sting your mouth.

● Avoid rough textured food like toast or raw vegetables as they can scrape at sore skin.

● Keep your food moist with sauces and gravies.

● Try drinking through a straw.

● Pineapple chunks clean the mouth and are refreshing.

- Tell your doctor about it. He or she can prescribe soothing or antiseptic lotions for you.

- Ask your doctor or nurse for advice about a suitable mouthwash. Mouthwashes can be very soothing, but many that you can buy may be too strong for you.

- Use a child's soft toothbrush to clean your teeth gently.

- If you wear dentures, leave them soaking in a denture-cleaning solution overnight and leave them out for as long as you can during the day to prevent them chafing your sore gums.

- If your tongue is 'coated' it may make your food taste unpleasant and might discourage you from eating. You can clean your tongue with a bicarbonate of soda solution: use one teaspoonful of bicarbonate of soda (available from your chemist) dissolved in a pint (60cl) of warm water. Clean your tongue with cotton wool dipped in this solution.

- Frequent drinks, even taking just a few sips at a time, can greatly help to keep your mouth moist. You may find fizzy drinks the most refreshing.

- Try sucking ice cubes or ice lollies. Home-made lollies can be easily made by freezing fresh juice in ice-cube trays or in special lolly containers with sticks which can be bought from many kitchenware shops.

- Moisten your food with lots of gravy or sauce.

- Avoid chocolate and pastry; they stick to the roof of your mouth.

- Sucking boiled sweets can stimulate your saliva; so can chewing gum.

- Try drinking a glass of sherry before a meal.

- *Salivix* boiled sweets (available on prescription from your doctor, and from most chemists) stimulate saliva.

- Tell your doctor about your mouth. He or she can prescribe artificial saliva sprays if you think they will help.

- Use lip balm for dry lips.

Has your taste changed?

Some people with cancer find that their taste changes, although most changes are only temporary. They may no longer enjoy certain foods or find that all foods taste the same, or they notice a metallic taste in their mouths after chemotherapy. Occasionally, they can't taste anything at all.

If you do have a change in taste, here are some tips for making your food more palatable:

● Concentrate on eating the foods that you like the taste of and ignore those that do not appeal to you. However, do try them again after a few weeks, as your taste may have returned to normal.

● Use seasonings and herbs like rosemary, basil and mint and spices to flavour your cooking.

● Try marinating meat in fruit juices or wine, or dress it in strong sauces like sweet and sour or curry. Cold meats may taste better garnished with pickle or chutney.

● Sharp-tasting foods like fresh fruit, fruit juices and bitter boiled sweets are refreshing and leave a pleasant taste in the mouth.

● Some people might go off the taste of tea or coffee. You could try a refreshing lemon tea instead or perhaps an ice-cold fizzy drink like lemonade.

● Some people find cold foods taste more palatable than hot foods.

● Serve fish, chicken and egg dishes with sauces.

This is the time to rely on quick convenience foods such as frozen meals, tinned foods, boil-in-the-bag meals and take-aways. Remember, though, to defrost frozen foods thoroughly and to cook all foods properly so as to avoid all risk of food poisoning. Read cooking instructions carefully and stick to them.

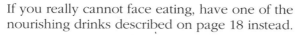

If you know in advance the times you are likely to feel tired, for example after radiotherapy treatment, then you could try to plan ahead to help you through these times. If you have a freezer, you could prepare food while you are feeling active and freeze it for when you are more tired. You could stock up on some of the convenience foods mentioned above. This is also a good opportunity to give friends and family the chance to help you by doing some shopping or cooking.

If you really cannot face eating, have one of the nourishing drinks described on page 18 instead.

If you feel you need more help coping at home with your eating, tell your family doctor (general practitioner) or contact the dietitian attached to your hospital. They may be able to arrange meals-on-wheels or a home help for you.

● Make sure you have plenty of fibre (roughage) in your diet. Good sources of fibre include wholewheat breakfast cereals like Weetabix or muesli, wholemeal bread and flour, brown rice, wholemeal pasta, fresh fruit and vegetables with skins on.

● Favourite natural remedies for constipation are syrup of figs, prunes and prune juice.

● Make sure you drink plenty of fluids. Hot drinks can be helpful. Some people find coffee is a powerful laxative.

● Gentle exercise will help to keep your bowels in working order.

● If the constipation persists, tell your doctor who can prescribe a laxative.

- While you have diarrhoea it is best to cut down on your fibre intake from fruit and vegetables.

- Make sure you drink plenty of fluids to replace the water lost with the diarrhoea, but avoid alcohol and coffee. Limit your intake of milk and milk-containing drinks.

- Eat small, frequent meals made from light foods – dairy produce, white fish, poultry, eggs (well cooked), white bread, pasta or rice. Avoid highly spiced or fatty foods and eat your meals slowly.

- Have your fruit stewed or tinned rather than fresh or dried. Bananas are 'binding'.

- If the diarrhoea persists, tell your doctor, who can prescribe some diarrhoea-relieving drugs for you, or consult a pharmacist.

- Eat and drink slowly. Take small mouthfuls and chew your food well.

- Avoid food that you think gives you wind; for example, beans, pickles and fizzy drinks.

- A favourite natural remedy is to drink two teaspoonfuls of peppermint water dissolved in a small cup of hot water. If you like, sweeten it with a teaspoonful of sugar.

- You could try taking charcoal tablets, available from your chemist.

- Gentle exercise, especially walking, can bring some relief.

- If the pain becomes severe or persistent, tell your doctor.

Feeling sick

- If the smell of cooking makes you feel sick, eat cold meals or food from the freezer that only needs heating up (but remember to defrost it thoroughly before cooking, and to make sure it is properly cooked).

- Alternatively, let someone else do the cooking!

- Avoid greasy, fatty or fried foods.

- Try eating some dry food, such as toast or crackers, first thing in the morning before you get up.

- When you feel sick, start off by eating light foods like thin soups or egg custards and gradually introduce small portions of your favourite foods, slowly building up to a more substantial diet.

- Sipping a fizzy drink is a popular remedy for feeling sick. Try mineral water, ginger ale, lemonade or soda water and sip it slowly through a straw.

- Try having drinks between meals rather than with your food.

- Ask your doctor to prescribe you some anti-sickness tablets (anti-emetics).

Soft diets can become boring when people tend to rely on soup and ice cream. But with a little imagination and effort, a soft diet can be both appetising and nutritious.

The golden rule is to eat your favourite foods, but make changes which will soften them. For example, dress foods in interesting sauces and gravies, finely chop meat and vegetables and casserole or stew them, and cut the crusts off bread for softer sandwiches. If you have access to a blender you could blend or liquidise cooked foods.

There are several commercial products available that you may find helpful, both in terms of convenience and variety. These products can be obtained from your chemist. Your doctor may offer you a prescription for some of them.

SOME SOFT NUTRITIOUS FOODS

Home-made soups	Pasta dishes
Milk puddings	Pancakes
Scrambled eggs (well cooked)	Braised meat
	Egg custard
	Porridge
Poached or flaked fish in a sauce	Cottage cheese
	Grated cheese
Stewed or puréed fruit	Jelly made with milk
Shepherd's pie	Yogurts

- Eat a little as often as possible if you cannot face big meals. Try to have a small portion of food every two hours during the day.

- Tempt your taste buds by making your food look as attractive as possible. Put small portions on your plate and garnish the food with lemon, tomato or parsley.

- A glass of sherry or brandy half an hour before a meal is a good way of stimulating your appetite. Some people find a glass of wine with their meals helps their digestion.

- Keep snacks handy to nibble whenever you can. Bags of nuts, crisps, dried fruit or a bowl of grated cheese are quite light and tasty. If these are hard for you to swallow, a yogurt or fromage frais may slip down more easily.

- Sweet or savoury nourishing drinks can be used to replace small meals (see page 18).

- Eat your meals slowly, chew the food well and relax for a little while after each meal.

- Sometimes the smell of food cooking can be appetising, but occasionally it can put you off eating. If cooking smells ruin your appetite, keep away from the kitchen and ask your family or friends to cook, or eat cold foods attractively presented.

- Everyone's appetite fluctuates between good and bad days. Make the most of the good days by eating well and treating yourself to your favourite foods.

- Have your meals in a room where you feel relaxed and without distractions.

Special eating problems

Some people with cancer may have special eating problems that are not covered by this booklet. For example, people with a colostomy or ileostomy or laryngectomy need to follow a special diet individually designed for them. Advice about these diets can be obtained from your doctor or dietitian.

You can also contact the organisations below:

The British Colostomy Association
15 Station Road
Reading, Berkshire RG1 1LG
Tel: 0118 939 1537

IA-The Ileostomy and Internal Pouch
  Support Group
Amblehurst House
PO Box 23
Mansfield, Nottingham NG18 4TT
Tel: 01623 628099

Oesophageal Patients Association
David Kirby (Chairman)
16 Whitefields Crescent
Solihull, West Midlands B91 3NU
Tel: 0121 704 9860

National Association of Laryngectomy Clubs
Ground Floor
6 Rickett Street, London SW6 1RU
Tel: 0171 381 9993

British Diabetic Association
10 Queen Anne Street, London W1M 0BD
Tel: 0171 636 6112

PART THREE
A healthy eating guide

So far, this booklet has dealt with the eating problems of people with cancer who have lost weight or have poor appetites. However, there are many people with cancer who never lose weight or have any difficulties with eating. For others, eating problems are only a temporary effect of their treatment and most of the time they can eat well.

This Healthy Eating section is sound nutritional advice for people with cancer, but with no weight loss or eating problems, or for anyone without eating problems who wants to follow a healthy diet, live a fuller life and feel better. In the long term, this diet may reduce the chances of getting heart disease and diabetes as well as certain types of cancer.

Some of the advice given in this section may seem to contradict that given in the Building-up Diet in Part One. The advice there is for specific groups of people with cancer who are eating very little or are losing weight and is not recommended for people who can eat normally.

Recently, there have been several reports concerned with improving the diet of people in Britain. The following section is a summary of that advice.

Try to maintain your weight within the normal range for your height (your family doctor can advise you on your normal weight). If you are overweight, reduce your energy intake by eating less fat and sugary foods. This allows your body to use up its surplus energy which is stored as fat.

Eat less fat

Many experts agree that in Britain we eat too much fatty food. Instead of getting our energy from starchy foods like bread and potatoes, we rely too much on animal fats such as red meat, eggs, butter and cheese.

What you can do to eat less fat

● Eat more fish and poultry rather than red meat.

● Choose lean cuts of meat and trim off all the fat you can. Remove the skin from poultry.

● Eat less fried food – bake, grill, steam or poach food instead.

●. Buy skimmed or semi-skimmed milk.

● Try the low-fat varieties of margarine, butter, yogurt and cheese.

● Cut out or reduce the number of fatty take-aways (e.g. fish and chips, burgers, sausages) that you eat.

● Avoid snacks which are high in fat, such as crisps and biscuits.

Eat more vegetables, fruit and cereals

Vegetables, fruit and cereals are all rich in fibre and vitamins. Fibre is sometimes called roughage. It is the part of the food which passes through the body without being completely absorbed, and keeps the gut healthy.

Some experts say we should be eating half as much fibre again as we eat now.

Try to eat fresh fruit and vegetables each day, particularly dark green and dark yellow vegetables like spinach, broccoli and carrots.

High-fibre foods

- Fresh fruit with the skins left on where possible.

- Fresh vegetables, including potatoes, especially with the skins left on.

- Wholegrain cereals, for example, brown rice.

- Wholemeal pasta and noodles.

- Wholemeal bread.

- Dried fruit, especially prunes.

- High fibre breakfast cereals like muesli, Weetabix, bran flakes or porridge.

Cut down on sugar

Sugar contains no useful nutrients apart from energy and we can get all the energy we need from healthier sources. In Britain we consume 84lbs (38kg) of sugar per person per year! Most of this is unnecessary and is partly responsible for tooth decay and obesity.

- Learn to do without sugar in hot drinks or switch to an artificial sweetener.

- Cut down on cakes, sweets and chocolates.

- Have fresh fruit instead of puddings. Sweeten stewed fruit with sweeteners.

- Choose foods with less or no added sugar, for example: tinned fruit in natural juices and low calorie drinks. Try sugar-free jellies, diet yogurt.

Cut down on salt

Most people eat much more salt than they need. Most foods are salted during cooking and manufactured foods contain a lot of added salt. Some experts say we should all aim to cut down our overall salt intake by about a quarter.

- Reduce the amount of salt in your cooking and try to avoid adding it at the table.

- Cut down on snacks with a high salt content like crisps or salted nuts.

- Try to use low salt manufactured products, and low salt or unsalted butter or spreads.

What about alternative diets for treating cancer?

Alternative diets for treating cancer have received much publicity over the past few years. You may have heard about diets that advise people with cancer not to eat meat and suggest drinking large amounts of carrot juice. Some recommend taking large doses of vitamins. (See page 8 for details on the use of vitamins.)

Many dramatic claims for cures of people with advanced cancer have been made and it is completely understandable that people with cancer should be attracted to diets which offer the hope of a cure. However, there is no scientific evidence that these diets cause the cancer to shrink, increase a person's chance of survival or indeed cure the disease. As these diets have not as yet been properly studied, their real effect is uncertain.

Some people do get pleasure and satisfaction from preparing these special diets, but others find them quite boring and even unpleasant to eat and time-consuming to prepare. A further problem is that some of the alternative diets are very expensive, and some can cause people to lose a lot of weight.

It can be very confusing to be faced with conflicting advice about what to eat, but most doctors recommend a well-balanced diet and one that you enjoy, as described in this booklet.

If you have any queries about these diets or are thinking of following one, ask your doctor's or dietitian's advice.

Cancer: recipes for health (2nd edn)
Clare Shaw and Maureen Hunter
Thorsons, 1995
ISBN 0-7225-3138-9   £5.99
As well as providing recipes, the authors look
at specific nutrients and their relation to cancer
and how to cope with weight loss, taste
changes etc. There is also a section on
encouraging children to eat.

*Non-chew cookbook
J. Randy Wilson
Wilson, 1985
ISBN 0-9616-2990-8
For people unable to chew food. Includes
recipes for soups, main dishes, vegetables and
desserts, as well as a section on basic nutrition.

Recipe ideas for commercial supplements
Nutricia Clinical Care
Ross Products Division
Fresenius Ltd
SHS International Ltd
Sutherland Health Ltd
Vitaflo Ltd.

Leaflets and booklets can be obtained by
writing to the relevant manufacturer
(addresses on page 45).

*This book is now out of print but may be
available from libraries.

Manufacturers of nutritional products

Fortisip, Fortijuce, Fortifresh,
Fortipudding, Fortimel, Polycal,
Protifar, Nutilis, Instant Carobel
Nutricia Clinical Care
Nutricia Ltd
White Horse Business Park
Newmarket Avenue
Trowbridge
Wiltshire
BA14 0XQ
Tel: 01225 711677

Calsip, Entera, Entera Fibre Plus,
Fresubin, Protein Forte, Provide
Xtra, Thick & Easy
Fresenius Ltd
Melbury Park
Clayton Road
Birchwood
Warrington
Cheshire
WA3 6FF
Tel: 01925 898000

Complan
H J Heinz & Co Ltd
Hayes Park
Hayes
Middlesex
UB4 8AL
Tel: 0181 573 7757

Build-up, Caloreen, Emelis,
Nestargel
Nestlé Clinical Nutrition
St George's House
Croydon
Surrey
CR9 1NR
Tel: 0181 667 5130

Enlive, Ensure, Ensure Plus,
Formance, Polycose, Promod
Ross Products Division
Abbott Laboratories Ltd
Abbott House
Norden Road
Maidenhead
Berkshire SL6 4XE
Tel: 01628 773355

Calogen, Duocal, Elemental 028,
Emsogen, Maxijul, Maxijul
Liquid, Maxipro, Maxisorb,
Scandishake
SHS International Ltd
100 Wavertree Boulevard
Wavertree Technology Park
Liverpool L7 9PT
Tel: 0151 228 8161

Hycal
SmithKline Beecham
Consumer Healthcare
SB House
Great West Road
Brentford
Middlesex TW8 9BD
Tel: 01753 533433

Thixo-D
Sutherland Health Ltd
Unit 1, Rivermead
Pipers Way
Thatcham
Berkshire RG13 4EP
Tel: 01635 874488

Vitajoule, Vitapro, Vitaquick
Vitaflo Ltd
6 Moss Street
Paisley PA1 1BJ
Tel: 0800 515174

Information

Provides information on all aspects of cancer and its treatment and on the practical and emotional problems of living with the illness. Information is on computer about services available to cancer patients, treatment and research centres, support groups, therapists, counsellors, financial assistance, insurance, mortgages and home nursing services. Some of these are listed on the following pages.

If you would like any other help, you can phone and speak to one of our experienced cancer nurses. The information service is open to telephone enquiries from 9am to 7pm Monday to Friday.

The number to call is 0171 613 2121 or you can call free of charge on 0800 18 11 99.

Counselling

Many people feel that counselling can help them deal with the problems of living with cancer. Counsellors use their skills to help people talk through the emotional difficulties linked to cancer. These are not always easy to talk about and are often hardest to share with those to whom you are closest. Talking with a trained counsellor who is not personally involved can help to untangle thoughts, feelings and ideas.

CancerBACUP's cancer counsellors can give information about local counselling services and can discuss with people whether counselling could be appropriate and helpful for them. CancerBACUP runs a one-to-one counselling service based at its London and Glasgow offices.

For more information about counselling, or to make an appointment, please ring 0171 696 9000 (London) or 0141 553 1553 (Glasgow).

Booklets

For a list of CancerBACUP booklets, or to order another CancerBACUP booklet, phone 0171 696 9003.

CancerBACUP booklets

Understanding cancer series:

Acute lymphoblastic leukaemia
Acute myeloblastic leukaemia
Bladder
Bone cancer – primary
Bone cancer – secondary
Brain tumours
Breast – primary
Breast – secondary
Cervical smears
Cervix
Chronic lymphocytic leukaemia
Chronic myeloid leukaemia
Colon and rectum
Hodgkin's disease
Kaposi's sarcoma
Kidney
Larynx
Liver

Lung
Lymphoedema
Malignant melanoma
Mouth and throat
Myeloma
Non-Hodgkin's lymphoma
Oesophagus
Ovary
Pancreas
Prostate
Skin
Soft tissue sarcomas
Stomach
Testes
Thyroid
Uterus
Vulva

Understanding treatment series:

Bone marrow and stem cell
transplants
Breast reconstruction
Chemotherapy

Clinical trials
Radiotherapy
Tamoxifen factsheet

Living with cancer series:

Complementary therapies
  and cancer
Coping at home: caring for
someone with advanced cancer
Coping with hair loss
Diet and the cancer patient .
Facing the challenge of
  advanced cancer
Feeling better: controlling pain
  and other symptoms of cancer
Lost for words: how to talk to
someone with cancer

Sexuality and cancer
What do I tell the children?
  – a guide for a parent with
  cancer
What now? Adjusting to life after
  cancer
Who can ever understand?
  – talking about your cancer
Will power – a step-by-step
guide to making or changing
your will

Notes